The Sage

By
Ronald Dowd

Copyright

The Sage

Remyrocks Publishing

ISBN 978-1-304-53035-6

1. The Path to Wisdom and Fulfillment

People have a need for health, wellbeing and purpose. They feel the need to contribute to the community in a way that is meaningful to them and others. The mature individual, or sage possesses a portfolio of life that contains pathways of opportunities and challenges. The portfolio advances the idea of maturity and provides tools to discover and develop capabilities and pathways to fulfillment. The key to opening the door to this path is found in the capacity of the human system to integrate all of its parts into a smoothly functioning mechanism for creating harmony and peace.

People are systems. People also organize into groups that function like systems. The personal human system is made up of three related subsystems that makes it whole and work together to make everything perform in all the right ways. These are the physical, mental and spiritual subsystems.

The physical subsystem is material and tangible. You can see and touch the parts. You have good physical health if you have all of the essential parts in each subsystem, and each part is playing its rightful role in an optimal way and working together with other parts in a smooth and effective manner.

The mental subsystem is psychological and intangible. You cannot see and touch the parts. But, you can feel them. There are two subsystems here; one having to do with sense, or intelligence, and the other with sensibility, or intuition. A well functioning mental system would result in perception, understanding and sensitivity, among other qualities.

The spiritual subsystem is the essence of being. It is not tangible. It is not the mind. It is the core of the human system. There is only one subsystem here, and it gives bearing to the others. Essence has to do with soul, values and temperament as major parts. Passion comes from here.

The physical subsystem provides substance to the body, the mental subsystem provides substance to the mind and the spiritual subsystem provides the glue that binds them together.

It is important that all of our systems are in good working order and that they work together in a synergistic or harmonious way. You have synergy when everything is running smoothly. When all subsystems and all of the parts are performing synergistically; you are whole. A synergistic system is one that achieves its purpose completely and with passion. Passion is the emotional energy that makes synergy possible.

You can play a piece on the guitar and not miss a note, but also not put any feeling into it. The audience will acknowledge your success with some applause. Allow passion to drive your performance and you might have a standing ovation. Now, the audience plays a role here also. An attentive and appreciative audience is more likely to give a standing ovation than one that is disinterested or alienated.

A system is more likely to bond with another system when both have some common desired goal. If the gifted guitarist and the audience both desire a superb performance, expect it and are passionate about it, then a standing ovation is more likely than not.

Relationships are the key. Making connections, building rapport and linkages and having empathy are the things that make for passionate relationships.

Artists and performers do this when their creative work provides both excitement and understanding of what has been created. Recognition of a brilliant and inspired performance is a celebration for all involved. Everyone feels justified and fulfilled.

Passion is the emotional energy that makes synergy possible. Without it your system is lacking and not performing in an optimal fashion.

Passion comes from within. You can't learn it from a book. Your doctor can't give you a prescription for it. It is not bestowed on a person because of status or position. It is an act of personal will. It comes from the essence of a person. The spiritual system has it as one of its parts. It's up to you to find it and spring it loose

Each of us needs to discover and develop his or her capabilities and pathways as the means to bring about our wholeness.

A good way to do this is to acquire wisdom, cultivate and sustain that wisdom and share that wisdom with others. Wisdom involves, as a core value, continuous learning to improve the quality of existence. A wise person will do several important things.

Have an attitude of service to others;
Consider others as equals;
Praise, rather than criticize others;
Be fair and reasonable in expectations of others;
Accept the reality of the situation;
Be open and sensitive to the environment;
Learn what is expected and pay attention to business;
Be sincere and show appreciation for others' interests, and
Relate to a greater cause or purpose.

A sage is a wise person, who is mature and has balanced presence and outward perspective. A sage recognizes and cultivates potential and promise in self and others, has capacity and willingness to grow and develop, continuously learns, shares wisdom, and mentors others. A sage senses and embraces change, is intuitive, adaptable, optimistic and grounded in reality.

Being a sage means that one is constantly seeking a state of maturity leading to wholeness through bringing about harmony in the working of all parts of the human system and in the relationship of the parts. It is a journey, rather than a destination. The journey follows a path that will take the person in the direction of wisdom and fulfillment. A portfolio is a toolbox carried by the sage for use in finding directions and pathway selection.

Testing My System

People are made up of a whole bunch of smaller systems that work together inside to make everything perform in an all right ways. Being all right is important to us. If we are off, or not all right, then we feel bad and make everyone else around us feel bad.

It is very important that all of our smaller systems are in good working order and that they work together in a harmonious way. Harmony means synergy. You have synergy when everything runs smoothly and purposefully. A totally synergistic person is on top of the world. All is well. Nothing goes wrong.

How does one get synergy? How does one keep it? Do you have to have the genes for it, or can a person learn what it is and develop skills to make it happen? No doubt that some of us have genes that make it easier to get synergy, but mostly it is something that requires knowledge that can be acquired and applied in a practical manner.

A good starting point would be to learn as much about the human system as you can. This knowledge will then help to identify the factors that make for synergy. If you know what it is that causes synergy, you can work on the things that will bring it about.

These are the physical, mental and spiritual subsystems in the personal human system.

The physical subsystem is materiel and tangible. You can see and touch the parts. Most of the larger parts anyway. Parts can also be viewed as systems in their own right. The muscular system in the body has all the properties of any other system. Its parts can be seen in a book on human anatomy if you're interested in the details. Then there is the circulatory system, digestive system, nervous system, and so on. A potential outcome of this system would be good physical health, or wellness. If you have all of the essential parts of all of the essential bodily systems, and each part is playing its rightful role in an optimal way and working together with other parts in a smooth and effective manner, then you are in possession of a synergistic physical subsystem. You are well, and in touch, and on top of the world.

The mental subsystem is psychological and intangible. You cannot see and touch the parts. But, you can feel them. There are two subsystems here; one having to do with sense, and the other with sensibility. Some major parts included in sense would be intelligence, reasoning, understanding and thoughtfulness. Parts of sensibility would be common sense and emotion. A potential outcome of this system would be positive mental health. A well functioning mental system would result in perception, understanding and passion, among other qualities. You possess a synergistic mental subsystem. You feel great.

The spiritual subsystem is the essence of being. It is not tangible. It is not the mind. It is the core of the human system. There is only one subsystem here, and it gives bearing to the others. Essence has to do with soul, values and temperament as major parts. If the physical subsystem provides substance to the body and the mental subsystem provides substance to the mind, then the spiritual subsystem provides the glue that binds them together. Synergy is really spiritual in nature. It happens when there is a higher order goal that gives a person a reason for being. You not only feel great, but you are great.

Each subsystem is further made up of parts that must be present for a system to be complete. An incomplete system will not function properly; if it works at all. Try riding a bike without wheels sometime.

Each of the parts has a specific purpose. The purpose is to play a role in making the system work properly. The role a part plays is always goal oriented and dynamic. A bike wheel turns and contributes to movement which is the bike's purpose. The reason we ride a bike, other than for exercise, is to move from one place to another.

A part can be present in a system, but not function properly. It is not playing its role to the utmost. Such a part is performing in a suboptimal fashion; meaning that it could be doing much better. It is important that parts work at their highest level of functioning if the system is going to be synergistic. Otherwise, it would be like running with a sprained ankle.

A part can be present and functioning optimally, but not working together with other parts in a smooth and effective manner. Try playing a guitar that is not in tune. If the part's role is to produce a musical sound that is pleasant to the ear, then one out of tune string will have the effect of ruining the sound. This will also have the effect of making the whole musical piece an unpleasant experience.

A synergistic system is one that has all of its essential parts, with each part playing its rightful role in an optimal way and working together with other parts in a smooth and effective manner.

Knowing When Your System Works

A working system is one that is goal oriented and has a purpose. It is one that achieves its goal completely and with passion. Passion makes synergy possible.

This brings up another important dimension of systems. There are closed systems and there are open systems. A closed system is self contained and does not need anything from outside itself. An open system does. Open systems are organic and must relate, or interact, with their environment in order to function. Molecules are closed systems. Humans are open systems. All of our subsystems need to get something from outside and give something back. Likewise, each subsystem needs to get something and give back something. In other words, a whole person has subsystems that relate to each other and relate to other systems on the outside.

Things really get complicated from this point on. Just think about the other systems relating to people. Other people, the job, the neighborhood, school, church, the climate, government, and the healthcare system are only a few of them. It's tough enough to get mind, body and soul together. Doing that and balancing relations with other outside systems is a very tall order indeed. Being a human is not easy.

This is where passion comes into play. Passion is the glue that binds the linkages between and among systems. A system is more likely to bond with another system when both have some common desired goal. If the gifted guitarist and the audience both desire a superb performance, expect it and are passionate about it, then such a performance is more likely than not.

Synergy happens when all of the parts of a system share a common goal or purpose and the parts are working together in relationship with each other in a smooth and effective manner. This state of affairs occurs when essential relationships are motivated by passion. In other words, passion of purpose is the reason the parts work together well. Passion is the emotional energy that makes synergy possible. Without passion, your system is lacking something special.

Each of us needs to discover and develop his or her capabilities and pathways as the means to bring about synergy. A good way to do this is to acquire wisdom, cultivate and sustain that wisdom and share that wisdom with others. Wisdom involves, as a core value, continuous learning to improve the quality of existence. The sum of this will be included in your life's portfolio.

How do we go about getting this wisdom? What kind of wisdom should we seek?

The acquisition of wisdom is no easy task. First of all, you need to acquire knowledge. This means learning. Not rote learning, by memorizing everything, but learning to understand and appreciate; mostly through gathering life experiences. Wisdom comes about through development of the four primary attributes of sense, sensibility, spirituality and skill

The Four S Attributes

Sense relates to the idea of intelligence or reasoning and understanding. We have the capacity to employ the mind's cognitive functions to make decisions and come to conclusions on the basis of logic, rationality and the scientific approach.

Sensibility relates to the idea of common sense or intuition and judgment. We have the capacity to temper logic and rationality with values that draw upon experience and environmental influences. The values of empathy and connectivity are particularly important here.

Spirituality relates to the idea of essence or soul and compassion. We are grounded in a frame of reference that continually recognizes the existence of other systems important to survival and success. Recognition of the significance of higher order systems is particularly relevant here.

Skill relates to the idea of competence or potential and ability. We are capable of managing and directing ourselves in a manner that gives full expression to physical and mental proficiency and aptitude.

The remainder of this book will be devoted to an in depth exploration of each of the four primary attributes and their significance to the sage in the pursuit of wisdom and fulfillment.

2. Developing the Attribute of Sense

As we know; sense has to do with intelligence; or reasoning and understanding. A human system has the capacity to employ the mind's cognitive functions to make decisions and come to conclusions on the basis of logic, rationality and the scientific approach. Systems thinking and analysis is a natural approach to expanding one's capacity to reason in a logical and sensible manner.

Systems thinking can serve as an invaluable tool for the sage in the pursuit of wisdom and fulfillment. It's wise to know as much about systems thinking as possible.

A system is essentially a combination of parts or components that form a unitary, inter-related whole. There are natural systems and there are synthetic systems. Natural systems occur in nature, and synthetic systems created by humans. Organizations and institutions are synthetic and designed by humans with a specific purpose, or mission in mind. A system can be anything that we are capable of imagining or seeing. Every system keeps itself going by sustaining a smooth, reciprocating interaction of its parts. Systems are always searching for ways and means to achieve perfection and will not rest until this happens. It hardly ever happens, of course, and so systems are continually striving to reach a state of affairs that may or may not be attainable. This is not as bad as it seems. After all; it's the journey that is important here. That's really the fun part. Notice that after the celebration of achieving success in a worthy effort, people will get bored soon thereafter, and start looking for a new challenge.

A system strives for balance and stability, or equilibrium. All systems have a need to be efficient, effective and synergistic. They all strive for perfection, or wholeness. Wholeness in a system means that it is functioning in a manner that achieves maximum production and results with minimum energy or resource commitment. Wholeness goes beyond just efficiency and effectiveness, however. It includes equilibrium, or the achievement of these in a manner that is harmonious and synergistic.

Synergy happens when the combined action of two or more system parts is greater than the sum of their effects individually. The smooth and mutually reciprocating functioning of all of the system's parts is essential for wholeness. When this occurs in nature, we can observe and authenticate what is seen. A vibrant, healthy athlete running a race conveys an image of beauty and wholeness. Likewise, the view of a snow-capped mountain on a clear and pleasant day conveys the same feeling. Synthetic systems, on the other hand require a design that defines the characteristics of wholeness and a blueprint for the construction and operation of the system.

For example, government is a system that takes a great deal of thought and energy to create and maintain. American government came from revolution and compromise. The United States of America is made up of individual state governments, each being a system in its own right. The states are combined into a larger system that is the federal government. The blueprint for this is found in the Constitution of the United States where the powers and obligations of the states and the federal government are defined. The purpose of the United States government is to form a more perfect union, maintain a system of justice, insure domestic tranquility, provide for a common defense and promote the general welfare of Americans. The part that has to do with forming a more perfect union is the most challenging. This requires the smooth and mutually reciprocating functioning of all of the states in the federal system. Sometimes this happens to a greater extent than in other times; sometimes not.

The Working of Systems

Most systems are open systems and draw on other systems for resources, transform these and return the results to them. All systems have structure, process and results. Structure has to do with architecture, or construction – the building blocks of the system.

A system's structure consists of inputs that come from the system's environment, usually from other systems. Inputs are resources used by the system to produce results. Production is brought about through the transformation of resources through a process, or a set of activities that serve to move the system to goal achievement. Production consists of process, designed and sustained by purpose. The human circulatory system moves blood through the rest of the human system so that we can live and breathe. The legislative branch of the federal government channels ideas and policies designed to bring about a more perfect union through production of laws. Results come in the form of outputs and outcomes. Outputs are tangible and relatively easy to define. Outcomes are not and may be almost impossible to define. Blood pressure is a well known measure of circulatory system performance. Almost everybody knows what it means and how to obtain measurements of blood pressure. Every drug store has a machine that is easy to use and gives readings for free. There is no agreement about what constitutes a more perfect union. Every election held in the United States of America is driven by rhetoric that attempts to define the meaning of good government in terms of the values and preferences of the candidates. These values and preferences change over time, so that it is unlikely that there will ever be consensus that will serve all generations of Americans.

Here is how a system works. Resources come from the environment and other systems and are introduced into the host system either through natural or manufactured mechanisms. Resources that are not accepted are discarded into other surrounding systems. Those that remain are embraced by the host system and incorporated into a process that transforms the resource into a product or other result that helps achieve the purpose of the system. A system's process is made up of activities, or functions designed to produce those outputs or results related to the system's goals.

Some examples of a system would be an atom, molecule, cell, organ, person, community, organization, state, nation, world and universe, in increasing levels of complexity. You will no doubt notice that some of these are found in nature and some are not. Naturally occurring systems evolve through the forces of nature and are not determined by us, although human behavior and actions do influence the course of nature at times. Systems that are brought about by human design, on the other hand, are there because we invented them. These are organizational systems for the most part that come about because we have a need to achieve a goal or result that has value to us. Communities, businesses, churches, governments and other forms of human organization are created by us to meet specific needs at some point in time during the journey of life and history.

Human organizations include individual persons or groups of persons. Individuals are the end result of a birthing process that begins with conception inside the womb and produces an offspring at the termination of pregnancy. The human system is a viable, open system that is sustained and nurtured by the continual interaction of mind, body and soul working in concert to give full expression to the four primary attributes of sense, sensibility, spirituality and skill.

The Role of Logic

It is evident that systems are very complicated, and require some effort to understand and apply by the sage as an attribute in the pursuit of wisdom and fulfillment. Sometimes it is helpful to visualize something as an abstract idea or model. A logic model is a systematic and visual way to see the structure and workings of a system and improve understanding of the relationships among system parts. A simple and straightforward model would begin with identifying system assets, or resources, and view what is done with them and the changes or results hoped to be accomplished.

Human and organizational behavior and actions are driven by needs and other inputs. The inputs are converted to resources that are available for work or production through activities. Planned activities are processes, programs and policies that guide implementation of work or production leading to the achievement of goals and objectives. Implementation of planned activities results in system outputs, or products of activities, and outcomes that change the nature or quality of the system. All of this can be visualized with the aid a logic model. A logic model follows the format of the rational thought process used by scientists and philosophers alike when they attempt to solve problems. There is a generic thinking progression normally employed here. It goes like this:

Assess the Situation - what is the specific problem or need that I am trying to address?
Set Goals - what has to be done to solve the problem or meet the need?
Analyze Alternatives - are there different ways to do this?
Select Best Alternative - which one is the best alternative?
Implement Plan - how can I proceed to achieve the goal?
Evaluate Results - how will I know when and if I succeed?

It is important that we think in an orderly and logical way if the pathway to wisdom and fulfillment is to be fruitful. Failure to think this way can lead us off the path and into side roads that could be frustrating and bewildering. For openers, there can be no true success unless it is defined ahead of time. Otherwise, how do you know you have it? Success needs to be envisioned by the person or group in terms of their needs. It's the needs that determine the goals, and the goals determine the plan of action. Unless you do a complete job of needs assessment; you will probably head down the wrong path – a path that leads either nowhere or to a place you may not want to go. Wandering aimlessly about is never a pleasant experience. Every system needs efficiency, effectiveness and synergy along with clear and unambiguous direction.

Assessing System Functioning

A sensible approach is systems analysis - a logical way to examine any system to determine how well it is working. Systems analysis involves examination of the structure, features and operation of a system with objectivity and recognition of the open and reciprocating nature of systems. This means that all of the significant components of the system and their essential relationships to each other should be considered. There needs to be recognition of the dynamic nature of systems and that they are goal oriented and time sensitive. A comprehensive assessment of a system requires a diversity of perspectives. Other people, within and outside human systems should be included in the analysis. There are different levels of systems analysis. A complete and comprehensive systems analysis will include assessment at all of these levels.

Activity - is anything happening? How many heartbeats are there every minute? How many laws has the legislative body passed?

Meeting Standards - are things happening according to established and accepted criteria? Are the numbers of heartbeats within the accepted range? Has the legislature passed too many or too few laws?

Efficiency - have results been achieved with minimal resources? How long does it take for the heart rate to return to normal after exercise? How many laws were stalled because of a filibuster?

Effectiveness - have results been achieved in an economical and timely manner? Does the heart rate perform adequately at various levels of exercise? Have the laws considered by the legislature addressed critical issues as seen in the eyes of the electorate?

Outcome - have intended results been produced? Was the runner successful in completing the race without cardiac event? Did the laws pass by the legislature adequately meet significant needs of the population?

Benefit - have results contributed to the overall value of the system or other systems? Did the heart rate performance help the runner finish the race in good time? Have the laws passed assisted the nation in its pursuit of happiness?

3. Developing the Attribute of Sensibility

Sensibility relates to the idea of common sense or intuition and judgment. A human system has the capacity to temper logic and rationality with values that draw upon experience and environmental influences. The values of management acumen and connectivity are particularly important here. Management and leadership are key qualities of the sensible person.

These values are in play when experience and environmental influences are garnered and systematically ordered to create purposeful structure in the life of an individual. The creation of structure is seen as an ongoing management process that helps us focus on the steps in our journey in a common sense and practical manner. A well ordered management process is very useful here.

It's very helpful to view management like you would any other system. A systems view of the practice of management helps to bind together all of the pieces needed to bring about synergy and wholeness, and smooth the passage to fulfillment.

Management system inputs include important resources and other supporting elements such as communication flow, planning and control mechanisms, decision-making venues, directing and organization styles and approaches, and defined roles and accountabilities.

Management system process includes important activities such as listening and asking questions, sharing ideas and feelings, group problem solving, conflict resolution, participation and involvement, acceptance, empathy and teamwork.

Finally, management system outputs and outcomes include results that lead to improved physical, mental and spiritual functioning through the full and unfettered expression of the four primary attributes of sense, sensibility, spirituality and skill.

The ultimate outcome of the human system is the acquisition of wisdom. Wisdom involves continuous learning to improve the quality of individual existence through maturity, balanced presence, and outward perspective. Recognition and cultivation of potential and promise in self and others, capacity and willingness to grow and develop, and continuous learning and sharing are all key features of sensibility.

Management at Work

Management is a process for accomplishing personal and group goals by working with others and through practicing the functions of planning, organizing, directing and controlling.

Planning is predetermining a course of action. This includes activities such as developing goals and objectives, formulating mission, visioning, scheduling, budgeting and developing policies and procedures

Organizing is arranging and relating tasks so that they can be performed efficiently and effectively. This would include designing jobs and tasks, putting together organizational structure and organizational relationships.

Directing is influencing people to perform and take effective action. This would include communication, decision-making, motivation, selection and development of team members.

Controlling is assessing results and regulating work in progress. This would include measurement, evaluating performance standards, correcting performance and monitoring benchmarks.

All of this can be learned. There are many books on the subjects of management and leadership, some academic and some in the popular genre.

Inputs to Management

Management systems, like all human systems, require resources and other supports in order to thrive. The activities required to sustain sense, sensibility, spirituality and skill are essential inputs to growth in humans. Human systems in modern societies need financial resources or the means to secure capital. Money is not everything. Money does not buy happiness, nor will it buy wholeness; but it helps. Lack of financial resources usually hurts and dampens the pursuit of happiness.

In addition to economic resources, human systems require supports that enable them to grow and prosper. System deterioration eventually leads to system demise. Supports enable growth through the provision of energy and fuel that feeds the mechanisms that drive the system.

Communication is the exchange of information among the parts of a system. In a human system, communication must be open, unfettered and clear in meaning if it is to be effective. Communication is effective when it leads to understanding. Understanding occurs when the meaning of information, feelings and thoughts is congruent with the listener's interpretation of message content and purpose. Meaning is greatly enhanced when a communication promotes harmony and is compatible with important values held by those on the receiving end, is not judgmental, is dynamic in terms of mutual goals, is thoughtful, empathetic and sensitive.

Planning and control mechanisms are system supports that allow predetermination of action and behavior through forethought. These mechanisms are cognitive in nature, and call upon the capacity of the human to employ logic and the rational thought process to plan and assess alternative strategies to system fulfillment. Logic models are useful here.

Decision-making venues are system supports that allow collective thought and deliberation through collaboration and systems interaction. These venues are both cognitive and emotional in nature, and look to the capacity of the human system to integrate logic and feeling to produce emotional intelligence through a process of interconnectedness.

Directing and organizing styles are system supports that allow the exercise of influence to work with and through other human systems to achieve goals. These styles are adaptations of the human system to situational factors presented by environments surrounding the system. These factors are power and value streams that require cognitive and emotional responses to achieve balance and maintain the course of the system. Leadership is all about the use of power, authority and influence to keep the system going.

Roles and accountabilities are system supports that define those qualities and characteristics that preserve equilibrium and allow smooth and harmonious functioning of all parts of the system. Roles and accountabilities make up the essence of the human system. Without them, there is no direction or path that leads to success or fulfillment. With them, the system has purpose, focus and a reason to survive.

The Process of Management

Management systems are dynamic. They are always on the move; transforming inputs in one way or another to produce outputs that lead to results. The process of transformation consists of those behaviors that facilitate the activities necessary to change resources and supports into effects. Behaviors such as listening and asking, sharing, problem solving, conflict resolution, participation and involvement, acceptance, empathy and teamwork provide the lubrication that enables the system to work.

Human systems are made up of people. Success in working with and through others requires understanding of what people need. People are motivated to participate and contribute to group activities if they are accepted, appreciated and approved by the group and their primary values are consistent with the group's values. The absence of acceptance, appreciation and approval creates a climate of distrust and skepticism that will disable the management process and lead to failure of the system. Inconsistency between individual and group values will have the same effect.

The key to organizing and sustaining a successful management process is effective leadership. Leadership is the exercise of power and influence to achieve system goals and objectives. Power is the potential to exert influence. The potential is acquired, nurtured and sustained by the person or group. Influence is the effect of the use of power on behavior. Power comes from legitimacy, reward or coercion, expertise and reference. Legitimacy happens when a person or group has authority conferred upon them by virtue of a charter of some sort. Most of us have this because we work in an organization that has job descriptions or we belong to a social unit such as the family, and have a title that confers legitimate status.

Rewards and punishments can occur through the granting or withholding of money, goods or services, gratitude, favors or advancements. The ultimate reward is belonging that comes through acceptance and appreciation. The ultimate punishment is banishment or isolation that comes through disapproval. Expert knowledge or skills are sources of power. We respect persons having a high level of these qualities, and are often persuaded by their logic and arguments, or emotional tenor. Finally, reference, or charisma is highly persuasive. No one can argue with the influential role of celebrity in most spheres of life. Political skill is the ability to use sources of power effectively to achieve political goals. Management skill is the same, but focuses on the achievement of individual and organizational goals.

The purpose of leadership is to bring about behavioral change in individuals or groups. The best way to bring about this change is for leadership to adopt an approach, or style that creates synergy throughout the system. Synergy occurs when leaders and followers dance to the same tune. This can happen when everyone knows what the tune is and are in agreement that they want to dance to that tune. Universal, mutual commitment to a common cause or goal is absolutely necessary for bringing about synergy and success.

How does a person or group secure and sustain effective leadership? First of all, there needs to be recognition of the culture of the individual or group and the degree of independence or submission on the part of the individual or group membership. Leadership must be cognizant of the values, customs, traditions, beliefs and philosophy of potential followers. Ignoring culture is to court disaster. Use of the different types of power and the extent of that usage must be tempered by knowledge of how followers will respond. The nature of response will be determined by follower acceptance of the use of power.

Most people accept the use of advertising to promote sales of services and products. Therefore, it is acceptable for us to purchase something on the basis of the influence of marketing campaigns. But this can only be carried so far. People are a highly independent lot and do not like to be "sold" on anything. We take great pride in our independence and freedom of choice. We allow ourselves to be influenced by advertising, but will not submit to it unconditionally. Ignoring the degree of independence or willingness to submit to influence of a person or group is to court further disaster.

Organizational culture is a reflection of follower propensities with respect to acceptance of leadership. Some cultures demand structure and a greater extent of direction in order to function effectively, while others want openness and independence of thought and action. Leadership that connects in a positive and mutually beneficial manner has the best chance of bringing about change in the desired direction.

A leader has a choice of styles that can be employed to achieve success. Leadership style falls along a continuum of tactics that are oppressive and dictatorial at one extreme and egalitarian and unrestricted at the other. The continuum runs from an entirely autocratic style by leaders inclined to be domineering in their relationships with followers, to an entirely participative style by leaders preferring to be more democratic in their approach. The style that works best depends on the situation. The autocratic style works best when the followers do not feel need to be independent, are not ready to assume responsibility, have little tolerance for ambiguity, do not feel that the issue or problem is very important, have little understanding or identification with the issue or problem, have limited knowledge of the issue or problem and are not at all interested or willing to share in the decision-making. The participative style works best when the opposite is true of the situation. There are very few situations that fall at either extreme. Most endeavors involve a mix of follower propensities and, therefore, require a combination of tactics in response to varying circumstances.

Management Results and Effectiveness

Since management is a process for accomplishing personal and group goals by working with and through others, and the ultimate goal of the human system is to acquire wisdom that empowers; system results need to be framed in terms of learning. Learning is a process that is continuous, deliberative, sharing and integrative. Enhanced sense, sensibility, spirituality and skill come about as a result of a conscious and deliberate effort to expand individual or group understanding of these qualities. Learning involves knowing. Knowing is knowledge of substance and process. Substantive knowledge relates to the human system's capacity to comprehend what is and process knowledge relates to the capacity to understand how.

Success in the management of human attributes relates to the ability of individuals and groups to engage in learning about sense, sensibility, spirituality and skill. Learning involves knowing "what" and knowing "how". Knowing "what" comes from knowledge of the subject and context of your area of interest. Knowing "how" comes from an understanding of the competencies required to realize change and goal achievement. Knowledge and skills, in combination, empower the person and organization to find success.

The accomplishment of life goals requires clear and relevant definition of your goals, a logic model that will plot a course and take you there within a reasonable time frame, and persistence to stay the course. You need to know how to move a system successfully through its paces by using common sense, devise and employ sound management processes, link to core values and use them to guide your progress throughout the journey.

4. Developing the Attribute of Spirituality

Spirituality relates to the idea of essence, or soul, and compassion. Healthy human systems continually recognize the existence of other systems important to survival and success. Recognition of the significance of higher order systems is particularly relevant in developing the attribute of spirituality.

A universal truth about the workings of the human system is that it is constantly in flux. What it is now is not what it was a moment ago. Some of this change occurs naturally with the passage of time and the events associated with time. These changes are input changes and present themselves regardless of the inclinations or preferences of the person or group. They are either ignored or dealt with in a more or less proactive manner. Ignoring change is a proactive strategy when it is employed deliberatively. Regardless of the response, change will happen and must be assimilated by the human system. Important issues here are how, when and how rapidly to change, how to effectively manage change, and how to determine system capacity for change.

The timing of change assimilation is critical for healthy systems growth and development. The spirit might be ready, but the other attributes may not be. There must be a balance among sense, sensibility, spirituality and skill in order to have system synergy. The human spirit orchestrates change. Effective system change management involves the coordinated employment of the other attributes. Change is brought about through leadership and management of the human attributes of sense, sensibility and skill. The human spirit provides the compass that integrates the other attributes in a manner that reflects the essence or core of the human system. An important dimension of change management is assessment of the readiness or capacity of the human system to accommodate change.

There are three basic types of change; incremental, tactical, and systemic. Incremental change involves performing minor modifications or incremental alterations. Tactical change involves introduction of new technologies and processes that are materially different from those currently in place in the system. Systemic change is the creation of new system performance expectations that requires innovative competencies, technologies and practices on the part of the system.

Incremental change strategies would embrace minimal adjustments that have the effect of fine-tuning one or more of the human faculties of reasoning, judgment or competence. This could mean that a person or group enrolls in a seminar to improve planning and analysis capability or learn to use a computer.

Tactical change strategies involve more extensive adjustments that have the effect of charting moderate variations to one or more of the alternative pathways embarked upon by the system to achieve success. This could amount to reshaping the manner in which a person or group makes decisions or exercises leadership, for example. An individual having a highly autocratic leadership style might make a shift to a highly democratic or participative style.

A systemic change involves major, significant transformation of the system itself. A political leader having been beholden to special interests in order to win elections who rejects that approach to politics would undergo a paradigm shift that amounts to a systemic change. Religious conversion of an individual is also an example of a systemic change in the human system. A losing team that learns how to generate synergy and becomes a winning team undergoes major systemic change.

Facing the Reality of Change

Change is never simple. Everyone knows the feeling of making a resolution to achieve a goal, or embarking on a course of action, and failing miserably. It seems that the spirit is willing but the flesh is weak. Success is never easy. The road to achievement is littered with all kinds of stumbling blocks and setbacks. Common barriers to change are cultural and learning impediments, technological impediments and measurement impediments.

Cultural and learning impediments usually include commitment to past practices that inhibit the ability to relearn. Everyone has run into the argument that "something can't be done" because it has never been done that way in the past. Individuals and groups owe their feeling of achievement to past experience and knowledge already in their possession. There is comfort and security in the past that the future does not seem to offer. This is a generalized fear of the unknown that all of us have. This fear serves the purpose of protecting ourselves from the ravages of uncertainty, and this can be a good thing. However, it also serves the purpose of hindering advancement and innovation and thus becomes a barrier to change. If change avoidance is a deliberate strategy, this can work to the advantage of a person or group. If change is in order, however, strategies need to be developed that lead to new knowledge and understanding to dissolve uncertainty, and chart a path to system balance and continued growth.

Technological impediments involve resistance to change because of the difficulties of mastering new methods or skills. Some of this relates to fear of the unknown due to doubt and hesitation, and some of this relates to difficulty in the use of untried technology. Nobody likes to make mistakes and technological change tends to be very threatening. It is difficult for people to accept that the road to success is paved with mistakes that come from trial and error.

Measurement impediments are those related to the inability to gauge progress or determine results. It is very easy to get lost, especially when the destination is unknown or vaguely defined. Although ignorance can be bliss, it is not at all satisfying to be continually in the dark. The assessment of progress and results can be severely hampered when there are nonexistent or inappropriate measures, misplaced, or limited emphasis on important measures. Measurement is a finely honed competency that needs to be learned and nurtured by the mature person.

Maturity and Wisdom

Maturity is wisdom that is cultivated, sustained and shared with others. Wisdom involves as a core value, continuous learning to improve the quality of human existence. Wisdom exists when an individual or group is in possession of sense, sensibility, spirituality and skill and exhibits the basic qualities of balance, potential, mentoring, capacity, learning and adaptability.

Balance occurs when the various parts of the system form a harmonious whole and not one of them is out of proportion nor is over emphasized at the expense of any other part. Potential is demonstrated when the person or group shows outward perspective and vision that allows future development or accomplishment. Mentoring is someone acting as coach or advisor to others as a means of support or empowering them to succeed. Capacity is the ability to remain open to new experiences and learning. Learning is continuous searching and acquisition of knowledge and skill for understanding and behavior change. Adaptability is the ability to adjust easily to changes and new conditions and to embrace the opportunities presented by change.

Group wisdom happens when a society, organization or institution embraces these same qualities and acts collectively to cultivate, sustain and share them with others. Fulfillment comes about through conscious and systematic advancement of all four human attributes of sense, sensibility, spirituality and skill. The sage learns to continuously strive for progress in all areas, and is driven by a spirit of tempered optimism and hope. The essence of the mature human system is compassion, love of learning, and improvement of self.

Collaboration is the Way to Go

Collaboration is a mutually beneficial and well-defined relationship entered into by two or more individuals or groups to achieve common goals. The relationship includes a jointly developed framework and shared responsibility for decisions and actions, mutual authority and accountability for success, and the sharing of vision and rewards.

A significant dimension of success in any endeavor is synergy that is brought about through working with and through others having a common purpose or vision. When a person or group consistently relates to a "higher power" that is greater than themselves, fertile ground is plowed that can produce larger dividends than a single individual or organization working alone. This higher power takes the form and shape of teamwork and serves to enlarge the power of the human system to perform. The human spirit is capable of relating to a higher order of systems, and is the driving force behind the formation and maintenance of collaboration.

Collaboration is also a process through which partners can constructively explore their differences and search for solutions that go beyond their own limited vision of what is possible. Collaborative synergy is the power to combine the perspectives, resources and skills of the partnership to accomplish objectives that cannot be brought about individually.

One way to find purpose is to develop a scenario that describes key features of the good life for you. Then figure out what you need to know and what you need to know how to do to have the good life you want. From there, you then need to identify important stakeholders who can help you find the good life. These stakeholders are key team members who will be crucial in your journey. Collaboration is the process that incorporates stakeholders' perspectives, values and support. Success is much more likely with them than without them. Finally, major barriers that have to be hurdled must be identified and addressed. Once the plan is in place, you are well on the road to realization of your unique good life. Best of all, because of the discipline used in mapping the journey, there is a good chance of knowing when you have arrived.

5. Developing the Attribute of Skill

Skill relates to the idea of competence, or ability. Skill in organizing and implementing a plan is essential for success in any endeavor. The difference between success and failure is usually due to weaknesses in the ability to carry out intentions. This is because the skill to execute planning is inadequate or absent. Power does not necessarily lead to influence or behavior change. There must be a conscious effort to activate the power before anything happens. You may have the power to reward someone, or yourself, but not carry through and actually do the rewarding. This has absolutely no effect. Possession of the attribute of skill does not bring success. Using it does.

The Importance of Finding Critical Life Issues

Critical issues are those super important, mega issues defined by the individual or group as being of major significance in efforts to accomplish goals and achieve success. These issues are critical because they represent opportunities or threats in the environment that might enhance or restrict capacity of the individual or group to exercise competencies necessary for survival and growth. These issues are identified through needs assessments and environmental scans, deliberate and rational thought, and systematic planning and evaluation. The purpose of identifying critical issues is to help the person or group refine its focus to specifically identify key challenges or life choices. It is important to clearly define the issues in terms of causes, boundaries, scope and dimensions, and the consequences to the individual or organization of not addressing the issue. Examples of some of these critical issues would include choice of alliances and partnerships, work and career, family, continuous learning and education, faith or religious affiliation.

Generic Thinking

There are six important steps that need to be undertaken in order for a person or group to move forward from identification of a critical issue to resolution and success. You will recognize these as the generic thinking progression discussed earlier.

1. Assess issues, problems and needs
2. Formulate goals and objectives
3. Design alternative paths to goal achievement
4. Examine alternatives and select the best path
5. Develop implementation plans
6. Evaluate progress and results

Assessing issues, problems and needs requires tools that take a person or group through a process of identification of the issue to be addressed, brainstorming about this issue through further identification of the underlying problems or needs associated with the issue, and coming to a consensus on the exact nature of the issue in terms of significance.

The process goes something like this. At your urging, a study group has been recently formed to address healthcare and social services for senior members of your community. The group has an initial meeting and brainstorms issues related to lack of access to healthcare and social services. The group decides to focus on the critical issue they refer to as "underserved frail elderly individuals". The group is now in a position to address a specific issue by progressing to the next step of the planning process.

Formulating goals and objectives involves expressing the issue in terms of its solution. The first step in the planning process has to do with asking the key question or questions needing to be answered. This step reframes the question as an answer, along the lines discussed below.

The purpose of this project is to provide access to healthcare, social and other support services for underserved frail elderly individuals. A key objective of the group will be to provide comprehensive, all-inclusive healthcare for all frail elderly persons in the community, and increase availability of accessible and affordable support services for this vulnerable population.

It is important that objectives be specific, quantifiable, reasonable and reflective of the community's priorities and values. The terms "comprehensive", "all-inclusive", "accessible", "affordable" and "availability" need to be defined in clear and specific terms to make them measurable. These definitions are necessary if one hopes to evaluate progress and success. Vagueness at this point in the planning process will only lead to uncertainty, and uncertainty will not allow the clear direction needed for sound planning and evaluation.

Designing alternative paths to goal achievement is an exercise in creative problem solving. Alternative programs, projects or other organizational paths to goal achievement need to be envisioned, articulated and evaluated in terms of the relative costs and benefits of each. Cost and benefit criteria can be measured as tangible or intangible. It is common practice to measure both cost and benefits in dollars and cents.

Other criteria can be employed, however. The possession of affordable health insurance, for example, would be a benefit measured by counting how many have it rather than the dollar value of the insurance. Increased rates of heart disease could be a cost of the lack of health insurance, as an indirect cost. Imagination is the only constraint here. Regardless of the measurement of costs and benefits, each viable and reasonable alternative needs to be identified and defined as a set of activities and actions that are designed to achieve the objectives established by the individual or group.

Criteria for assessment of the chosen alternatives should be developed in such a way as to reflect the values of the individual or group. These values need to be identified and articulated as well. Consensus is required because a group is involved. No significant values should be omitted. Ignoring a deeply held value by a group member can only lead to dissatisfaction with the planning process and frustration with the results. This leads to lack of support for the chosen path and will undermine any efforts to implement the plan and reduce the likelihood of success.

Examining alternatives and selecting the best path entails an analysis of the benefits and costs of each alternative pathway and selection of the best alternative in terms of the individual or group values chosen as criteria for decision-making. The alternative that produces the most benefit for the least amount of cost is the one selected for implementation. If this is not the case and the person or group selects a suboptimal alternative, something is missing in the analysis. An important criterion is at play, but not articulated for some reason. This is an acceptable decision as long as the criterion surfaces and is recognized and accepted by all concerned. If it is decided to hide the criterion for some reason, the issue will surface at some time in the future and most likely will subvert the project. This is true because hidden criteria represent values that need to be recognized and given place in the decision-making process lest they sizzle below the surface and erupt at a most inopportune time.

Developing implementation plans is a process that translates the selected alternative into a sequence of action steps that define a process comprised of resources, activities, accountabilities and milestones for measuring progress on goal achievement. There should be a clear and unmistakable lineage of thought that leads from the first step that initiates a project to the intended, specific results. Individuals and groups responsible for action steps need to be identified and incorporated into the implementation decision-making process. They need to know exactly what their responsibilities are and when they are expected to perform. Most implementation plans that fail do so because somebody either did not perform or did not know that they were supposed to perform. A plan stands little chance of success without a schedule of actions linked to responsible parties.

Evaluating progress and results requires the design of a flow of information that informs all responsible parties of the progress of activities intended to produce those outputs and outcomes required to successfully achieve project goals and objectives. Evaluation is a highly structured exercise that requires specificity in the delineation of goals and objectives, clear and unambiguous linkages between actions and activities and outcomes, and measures of progress and end results.

Putting Together a Portfolio

A portfolio is a package of interests, values and directions arranged to provide a structure that will guide behavior and actions leading to success in an area of endeavor. A complete and thorough portfolio analysis will include assessment of external and internal environmental forces and trends, clear and unmistakable issue identification, stakeholder analysis and development of directional strategies.

Timing is important because change is the order of the day, and needs may vary with the winds of that change as detected by environmental forces that set the stage for future directions. Timing is usually a long range phenomenon, but may be shorter if environmental forces shift rapidly. For example, a portfolio structured to accommodate retirement may need quick revision if a person's pension proceeds come up short of the financial requirements that would support a full retirement lifestyle. Suddenly, part-time employment may need to be added as a significant portion of the portfolio. Portfolios will normally correspond with organizational mission or vision for a group, and major life events for an individual. Business corporations always have a common mission to make money; usually measured in terms of profit. Individuals usually have life events that center on family, career, home, recreation, higher education and retirement.

A portfolio should include an organizational scheme for development and implementation of plans and strategic initiatives that need to be undertaken in order to succeed. Planning does not occur in a vacuum. A collaborative effort needs to be organized to insure that important stakeholders are involved from the start and remain involved until success is achieved. The ultimate success of any plan is determined by the concerted energy of committed stakeholders. The values and support of these stakeholders must be incorporated into the planning from the start, and the process underlying plan implementation must continually engage their active interest. This means that teamwork is an essential ingredient of successful portfolio development even though the portfolio is personal.

Implementation and Evaluation of Strategies

Implementation of strategies and plans requires a well thought out action plan that clearly identifies what has to occur if goals and objectives are to be realized. It's always a good idea to test and validate goals or objectives to provide for a reality test. This can be done on a virtual basis through scenario analyses that attempt to forecast results associated with various assumptions about the plan or strategy. Scenario analysis is a thought process capable of creating a more rational basis for determining if the objective can be reasonably accomplished within the time period projected. This analysis helps to assess that knowledge and skills necessary to carry out the plan are present in the individual or organization, the resources required are available or can be made available, all necessary information is known, or other alternatives that need to be considered. Since scenario analysis is entirely cognitive, there is no need to commit resources or take risks to discover barriers that might impede progress or spell disaster.

An action plan needs to provide detail on specific expected results, objectives and milestones, and responsibilities of all stakeholders involved in the planning process. In addition, there should be schedules of all activities, resource requirements and sources, an ongoing communication and review process, and procedures for accountability.

Evaluation should incorporate a logic model to provide focus on relationships among outcomes, outputs, activities, resources and barriers. A typical logic model used in evaluation would ask questions about the cause and effect relationships among resources, activities and results, and would try to explain those factors that could influence results or goals. Goals are associated with activities that led to results framed as questions expressed as measures of the results as either outputs or outcomes, or both. An example would be the following.

Evaluation Question - have the services been provided for the target population and at the levels specified and have the services produced the coverage specified?

Goal - provide comprehensive, all-inclusive healthcare and support services for all frail elderly individuals in the United States by the year 2015.

Activities - extend Medicare coverage of all-inclusive care to frail elderly persons who are poor and over the age of 80 years through traditional Medicare programs included under Part A, Part B and Part D of that legislation.

Develop and market plan to enroll sufficient numbers of the target population to achieve 95% coverage of eligible individuals not otherwise covered by other programs by the year 2015.

Output Measure - changes in enrollment of disabled elderly who are at or under the poverty level and over the age of 80 years. At least 95% of the eligible population will be enrolled by the year 2015.

Outcome Measure - changes in utilization of healthcare services by eligible persons who are enrolled in the program.

It is important to remember that the environment within which planning is implemented is dynamic. This means that evaluation needs to be flexible and may need to be changed as well. If the factors that influence results shift in a significant manner, then a change in thinking will occur. This will lead to modifications in the logic model and evaluation plan and perhaps in the plan itself. This means that it is important to always be on alert for significant shifts in the environment or the human system and be prepared to make whatever changes are necessary to support your vision for success.

Success and Failure

Success happens when you get what you want. This whole process began with an identification of problems or needs. You are successful when those problems are solved or the needs are met. The example given addressed the issue of health services for frail elderly persons. The planning and evaluation process would be exactly the same for a group or individual. Organizations are human systems, but they function in much the same way as individuals. They have structure, process and results. They measure success in the same way and keep track of environmental trends just like individuals' do. If they are adaptable enough to make adjustments in response to shifts in environmental trends, their chance of success is improved and their chance of failure is diminished. If not, there may be serious problems ahead. Likewise, the individual needs a good store of flexibility to make the grade.

Success is permanent. Failure is temporary. Always remember this and you will never have problems dealing with failure.

When something goes wrong and you think that you have deviated from the path; it's time to check the trail map to find out if something was missed or the wrong turn was taken. The trail map for each journey is the one developed in the portfolio discussed earlier. Checking means that each step in the planning process is examined to determine whether or not everything was done correctly. So that you don't forget, these steps are as follows.

Assess issues, problems and needs - Has the need been clearly identified and has consensus on its significance been reached with stakeholders?

Formulate goals and objectives - Does an objective make sense in terms of the problem to be addressed? Is it specific, measurable and reflective of stakeholder values?

Design alternative paths to goal achievement - Have all feasible alternatives been identified and articulated? Have criteria consistent with stakeholder's values been identified for use in evaluation of alternatives?

Examine alternatives and select best path - Have the criteria for evaluation of alternatives been faithfully applied to the analysis? Is there evidence of hidden criteria at play?

Develop implementation plans - Is the action plan and schedule complete so that important steps are not overlooked?

Evaluate progress and results - Has an evaluation plan been developed and followed to monitor progress and assess results of the plan?

6. Putting it all Together

The sage is on a continuous journey with rest stops along the way. The attainment of wisdom and fulfillment necessarily involves commitment to a set of processes that require adjustments along the road. There are bound to be setbacks and diversions that lead us off the path. It is up to us to know when this happens and have the will to get back on track.

A sage is a mature person who is regarded as being wise, knowledgeable and experienced in life. Wisdom and sound judgment are the hallmarks of the sage. Wisdom and judgment come from recognition of the importance of continuous learning about things and how to do things. The sage makes only one assumption in life – things will change; nothing stays the same.

The sage is an individual having a portfolio of life that contains opportunities and challenges to forge these pathways to wholeness. In order to do this, the individual needs to develop and nurture the capacity to integrate all of the parts of the human system into a smoothly functioning mechanism for creating harmony and peace. This means that there must be recognition of the nature and qualities of the three major parts of the human system. We know from earlier discussions that the physical subsystem is material and tangible. You can see and touch the parts. The mental subsystem is psychological and intangible. You cannot see and touch the parts. But, you can feel them. Finally, the spiritual subsystem is the essence of being and it gives bearing to the others.

Synergy and wholeness go together. Like love and marriage, synergistic performance of the human subsystems produces a wholeness that is more than the sum of the parts. It is an integrated system that works in harmony and moves to perfection. Passion is the lubrication that brings about a seamless interaction of the parts. It is the primary task of each of us to discover and develop the capabilities and pathways to bring about the wholeness that each of us wants and needs. The way to do this is by acquiring, cultivating and sustaining wisdom and then share that wisdom with others. Obtaining wisdom is a learning process. Sharing wisdom is a giving process. Since giving always provides greater rewards than receiving, sharing provides meaning and taps into the spiritual realm as the essence or core of life.

Continuous Learning Improvement

Wisdom comes about through development of an individual's primary attributes of sense, sensibility, spirituality and skill. Continuous learning is the way to develop and sustain these attributes. Learning has the effect of improving the human condition; not only at the individual level but the community level as well. Each of the four attributes should be cultivated so that there is balance among them in the human system. This will produce the synergy needed for a complete, wholesome and fulfilled person.

Sense relates to the idea of intelligence, or reasoning and understanding. Continuous learning here addresses our cognitive functions. Important subjects to study would include logic, science, philosophy, decision theory, religious thought, history and other liberal arts and sciences. A sage needs to have an insatiable appetite for reading and thoughtful deliberation.

Sensibility relates to the idea of common sense, or intuition and judgment. One can learn about the relationships among experience, environmental influences and the importance of human values in life. Methods to cultivate empathy and connectivity can be found and learned and applied in everyday life. In other words, one can figure out how to develop intuition and sound judgment that balances logic and common sense. The key to doing this is management. Management is a process for working with and through others to achieve goals or realize purpose. Management is a recognized discipline and can be learned.

Spirituality relates to the idea of essence, or soul and compassion. It is also possible to inquire into the nature of spirituality and learn about things of the soul. Human spirituality is a master frame of reference that links our senses and sensibilities into a set of values and principles that provide a moral compass that leads us in the right direction. Tapping into these basic values provides the passion required for our best performance as human systems. We learn about these values through the study of religion, law, ethics, and culture and through our life experiences. Although everything is in a constant state of change and adjustment, our spiritual compass is stable and unchanging.

Skill relates to the idea of competence, or potential and ability. Among all of the primary human attributes, skill stands out as the one most amenable to development through learning. It is not sufficient to possess competency. It must be activated or put to use before it can have any impact. Therefore, it becomes important to not only learn the methods and techniques that represent skills, but one must also learn how to use them to achieve action or accomplish results.

Improvement of the human condition will be greatly enhanced if an individual formulates, implements, and evaluates a portfolio of strategies designed to accomplish major goals. The same thinking applies to groups and organizations. Goals should address very significant needs or issues. Profitability is a major goal for businesses of all types. Indeed, profitability is the universal mission of these types of organizations. Promotion of the health and welfare of the population is a major goal of government and not for profit organizations. This is their mission.

Portfolios for organizations and businesses need to be developed to correspond to major strategic initiatives. These also need to be continually reviewed. Life is dynamic. It follows that change always should be anticipated and adjustments probably will need to be made to plans and strategies.

Putting Together a Life Portfolio

A synergistic system has all of its essential parts; with each part playing its rightful role in an optimal way and working together with other parts in harmony. The physical subsystem provides substance to the body, the mental subsystem provides substance to the mind and the spiritual subsystem provides the glue that binds them together. When all subsystems and all of the parts are performing synergistically; you are whole. Putting together a life portfolio involves development and implementation of strategies that will lead to wisdom. This, in turn will lead to paths that empower a person to mature in the structuring and expression of their primary attributes of sense, sensibility, spirituality and skill.

Strategies that lead to improvement in sense involve intelligence. Intelligence is the ability to think and learn. This boils down to reason and understanding. Improvement in reasoning and understanding happens when a person pursues a course of action that leads to the acquisition of knowledge. The pursuit of knowledge addresses the question – what do I want to know? Subject matter and context are important here. Knowledge of subject matter has to do with facts and information. Context provides the means to understand what you know. Understanding leads to wisdom. Strategies that lead to improvement in sensibility involve common sense. Common sense is the ability to exercise practical judgment, based on experience. This boils down to intuition and judgment. Improvement in intuition and judgment happens when effort is made to forge linkages between knowledge and experience and use them to make decisions or take action. The pursuit of common sense addresses the question – have I been down this road before? If so, how can I apply the lessons of the past to the needs of today? Linkages with the other primary attributes and time provide the methodology that allows sound judgment.

Strategies that lead to improvement in spirituality involve passion. Passion is intense emotion or feeling. This boils down to essence and compassion. Improvement in a person's essence is not possible. It is there. It just needs to be found and used to advance the human spirit and growth. This involves a deliberative process that "looks within" the individual and taps the inner strength to persevere. Tapping the inner strength produces the passion that is necessary for synergy.

Strategies that lead to improvement in skill involve competence. Competence is the capacity to do things. This boils down to potential and ability. All human systems have the potential to move toward wholeness or perfection. Some will get closer than others. The higher the level of ability, the closer to perfection a system can be. Knowing "how to" do something and applying this knowledge by taking action is the key to a skillful individual or group. Identifying needed skills and learning how to use them is important here.

Human systems are open systems. Each of the major subsystems (physical, mental and spiritual) is open as well. This means that we need to have interaction among our subsystems and with other systems outside of ourselves. Physical, mental and spiritual parts of the human system relate to each other, and their relationships are necessary for survival. In other words, each relies on the others for viability and wholeness. As you might recall, wholeness is when all parts of a system are performing synergistically. Figuring out what is important and working to balance interactions in a manner that brings about smooth and seamless operation of the human system is exceedingly difficult. The task is made tenable when it is understood that relationships are significant in making the connections required, and relationships are driven by passion which has its origin in the human spirit. We do not need to have all of the answers about the functioning of systems. All we really need to know is that the parts will come together if there is a common purpose among them. We just need to figure out what this is.

The Shape of Your System

The shape of your system can have an influence on how it functions. Some persons or organizations favor, or show preference for one attribute over another. The shape of a system indicates the relative strength of an attribute or combination of attributes that contribute to its success. In other words, synergy will vary from system to system in the mix of ingredients needed to provide full expression of any particular attribute. A person who is intellectually strong, emotionally mature and spiritual, but lacking in competency in important life areas can possess synergy. But, how can such a person achieve perfection and be whole? Discrepancies in competence can be covered by other systems through relationships. Collaboration and team work can enhance a system, bring about synergy and move a system towards wholeness.

Is your system square? A person with a square system tends to be firm, pragmatic, and responsible and value process and procedures. Planning and control are strong suits and activities like project management come naturally. The square person is most comfortable with an autocratic leadership style and will rely heavily on qualities of sense (intelligence) and skill (competency) to achieve goals.

Is your system round? A person with a round system is more likely to be abstract, aggressive, and methodical and value logic and knowledge. Policy and strategy are strong suits and strategic thinking comes naturally. The round person is most comfortable with a semi-autocratic leadership style and will rely heavily on qualities of sense (reasoning) and sensibility (intuition) to achieve goals.

Is your system oblong? A person with an oblong system tends to be compassionate, caring and animated and value ideas and creativity. Empathy and intuition are strong suits and the exercise of influence comes naturally. The oblong person is most comfortable with a participative leadership style and relies heavily on qualities of sensibility (passion) and spirituality (synergy) to achieve goals.

System shape is symbolic and not meant to be a representation of the actual configuration of any particular system. Its value is found in the association a person might have with their approach and style and the configuration and strength of their particular attributes. It could be said that a person has a square approach or style, a round approach or style, or an oblong approach or style, depending upon where they fit along the continuum of attributes.

System shape may not have any practical value in the pursuit of wisdom and fulfillment, but the allegorical association of commonly recognized objects fosters a deeper meaning of the idea of system and this allows greater intimacy with the human spirit. Spirituality is an essential system attribute and is indispensible to success.

Successful Traits for the Sage

The wise person or sage should possess the following traits for success.

Have an attitude of service to others. A sage has the capacity to suppress the ego and contain self-centeredness. A self-serving individual or organization will eventually be found out as lacking interest or concern with others. Selfishness will turn people away and they will not be inclined to participate in your journey. Losing important stakeholders is the same as losing yourself.

Consider others as equals. Do not think that others are of lesser stature or importance than you. Likewise, do not think that they are of greater stature or more important. This does not mean that someone with more authority or expertise should not be respected for these qualities. It means that all are equal as individuals or human systems

Praise, rather than criticize others. It is true that you can attract more flies with honey than with vinegar. Every person of sane mind will feel that praise is sweet. It is much more likely that praise will leave a good taste and bring positive reactions than the bitterness of criticism. Remember; the goal is to achieve success by working with others.

Be fair and reasonable in expectations of others. Fairness and equity are the ideas that allow the rule of law to work. The United States is a democracy that is governed by law. The rule of law applies to everyone, great and small. Our courts are expected to apply the law in a fair and reasonable manner; respecting the rights of the individual. Follow their lead and behave accordingly.

Accept the reality of the situation. You can only change what you can change. Accept this notion and try another path if the one you selected presents barrier that are unyielding.

Be open and sensitive to the environment. The human system is one among many. Environmental forces are capable of knocking you off course very quickly. Drive defensively and expect the unexpected at all times.

Learn what is expected and pay attention to business. Ask for clarification even though you think you know what is expected. Verification serves to reinforce memory, which can be very short-lived. The wise person will be prudent and attentive to detail. Remember, the devil is in the detail.

Be sincere and show appreciation for others' interests. Always try to put yourself in others' shoes. This will keep you honest and show that you are sensitive and a sincere person.

Relate to a greater cause or purpose. Belief in a high power or great cause is invaluable. Absent this; synergy is impossible and your employment of all of the primary attributes will produce limited results at best.

7. Some Practical Suggestions

A sage is a wise person, who is respected and mature, and has balanced presence and outward perspective. These qualities are based on the recognition and cultivation of potential and promise in self and others, and on the capacity and willingness of the sage to grow and develop, continuously learn and share wisdom, and mentor others. This is all easy to say; but very difficult to realize in life. Barriers presented by limitations of our physical, mental and spiritual subsystems are constantly and persistently reminding us of the reality of our capacity to achieve maturity as discussed and defined in this book. But; take heart. Remember that life is a journey. The journey is the most important part; and enjoyment of the pursuit of wisdom and fulfillment comes from the pleasure of the trip.

It is usually more fun to take a trip when you have a destination in mind and a roadmap that provides milestones and directions.

A destination is a highly personalized idea. Individuals and groups normally have many destinations throughout life. Groups and organizations are always formulated to achieve a purpose. The purpose then serves as a basis of multiple goals and objectives designed to accomplish the purpose. The overall purpose may not change over time; but goals and objectives need to be flexible and change in response to changing needs or requirements. Individuals, on the other hand, are born; not formulated by other individuals, like organizations. An individual will have a singular purpose to live to the fullest extent possible. The pursuit of happiness is deeply ingrained in the essence of each and every one of us.

Happiness is a state of being that will vary from one individual to another; but will have a common denominator of self actualization through the pursuit of wisdom and fulfillment as determined by each of us. Someone else's happiness will not be the same as yours. Their journey will be theirs. Yours will be yours. We share an interest in the free and personalized search for wisdom and fulfillment.

Freedom to embark on the journey is largely shaped by environmental factors. Americans have a great deal more freedom than persons living in many other nations. Wealthy individuals have more freedom than those living in poverty. Strong and healthy individuals have more than disabled or vulnerable individuals. All that can be said about this is that you do what you can with what you have. Make the best of your situation. It is truly amazing what an "underdog" can accomplish. Never give up. Stay in the game.

An organized and logical mind is very useful. There is a generic thinking progression normally employed by the human mind that makes the journey less stressful and more enjoyable. It goes like this:

1. Assess the Situation - what is the specific problem or need that I am trying to address?
2. Set Goals - what has to be done to solve the problem or meet the need?
3. Analyze Alternatives - are there different ways to do this?
4. Select Best Alternative - which one is the best alternative?
5. Implement Plan - how can I proceed to achieve the goal?
6. Evaluate Results - how will I know when and if I succeed

It has been mentioned that enjoyment of the pursuit of wisdom and fulfillment comes from the pleasure of the trip. A trip planned with forethought, and application of the thinking progression outlined above will be more enjoyable than one not planned or haphazardly started and executed. The first step of your journey will be to engage in a thoughtful exercise that results in a clear path to a fully articulated journey to a known, desired destination. The generic thinking progression will help you to do this.

If you view the journey and the road map as a system, then systems analysis methods can be employed to help determine how you are doing. There are different levels of systems analysis. A complete and comprehensive systems analysis will include assessment at six, separate but interdependent levels.

1. Activity - is anything happening?
2. Meeting Standards - are things happening according to established criteria?
3. Efficiency - have results been achieved with minimal resources?
4. Effectiveness - have results been achieved in an economical and timely manner?
5. Outcome - have intended results been produced?
6. Benefit - have results contributed to the overall value of life's journey?

It's important to keep on track, and know that you are towing the line. Continuous monitoring and evaluation of the progress of your journey does this.

The second step of your journey will be to work out a plan of action that includes major activities, milestones and results. This needs to be in sufficient detail to allow measurements, or soundings, as you move through the journey. Paying attention to, and developing metrics for each of the six levels will provide the satisfaction you need to tell how well things are going.

Life's journey can be viewed as a process that is made up of numerous parts in continuous motion. We don't live life sitting on a log; but are up and about constantly assessing our progress, making adjustments and setting new bearings. Every process needs to be managed. Therefore, it is useful to have some knowledge about management and have skill sets that enable us to intelligently administer the various aspects of our journey. Earlier, management was defined as a process for accomplishing personal and group goals by working with others and practicing the functions of planning, organizing, directing and controlling.

1. Planning - is the management function of predetermining a course of action.
2. Organizing - is the management function of arranging and relating tasks so that they can be performed efficiently and effectively.
3. Directing - is the management function of influencing people to perform and take effective action.
4. Controlling - is the management function of assessing results and regulating work in progress.

This is classic management. There are numerous books on the subject. Most of these are popular publications that appeal to a general audience. Many are textbooks, written by professors and meant to be educational tools. This book is not intended to be a textbook, but is meant to help you travel life's journey in the most pleasurable and satisfying manner possible. Some knowledge and skill in management should help.

The third step of your journey will be to arm yourself with some basic knowledge and skills about management and leadership. Talk to a librarian about books and other materials that will help you. Tell the librarian to keep it simple. Try for a basic understanding - no fluff or academic complexity.

Surely, you are aware by now that maturity is wisdom that is cultivated, sustained and shared with others. Wisdom involves, as a core value, continuous learning and six basic qualities.

1. Balance - the various parts of the human system form a harmonious whole and not one of them is out of proportion nor is over emphasized at the expense of any other.
2. Potential - the person or group shows outward perspective and vision that allows future development or accomplishment.
3. Mentoring - someone acting as coach or advisor to others as a means of support or empowering them to succeed.
4. Capacity - the ability to remain open to new experiences and learning.
5. Learning - continuous searching and acquisition of knowledge and skill for understanding and behavior change.
6. Adaptability - ability to adjust easily to changes and new conditions and to embrace the opportunities presented by change.

The fourth step of your journey is to acknowledge the six basic qualities. Do not forget these. They will get you through the rough spots and make for a more enjoyable and fruitful trip.

The four steps discussed here constitute useful tools of thought and action that will give you an advantage for success. A significant dimension of success is synergy that is brought about through working with and through others having a common purpose or vision. Don't forget; when a person or group consistently relates to a common cause that is greater than themselves, fertile ground is plowed that can produce larger dividends than a single individual or organization working alone. This takes the form and shape of collaborative partnerships and serves to enlarge the power of the human system to perform. Remember; collaborative synergy is the power to combine the perspectives, resources and skills of the partnership to accomplish objectives that cannot be brought about individually.

Finally; a portfolio is a package of interests, values and directions arranged at a point in time to provide guidance for a particular journey. Timing is important because needs may vary with environmental forces that may require adjustments in destination. Portfolios will normally correspond with organizational mission or vision for a group, and major life events for an individual. A portfolio should include plans and strategic initiatives that need to be undertaken in order to succeed. This includes provisions for collaboration to insure that important stakeholders are involved from the start and remain involved until success is achieved. The ultimate success of any plan is determined by the concerted energy of committed stakeholders. The values and support of these stakeholders must be incorporated into the planning from the start, and the process underlying plan implementation must continually engage their active interest. Teamwork is an essential ingredient of successful portfolio development, even though the portfolio is personal.

Remember that life is a journey and includes the presence and participation of others interested in your destination. The journey is the most important part; and enjoyment of the pursuit of wisdom and fulfillment comes from the pleasure of the trip.

www.ingramcontent.com/pod-product-compliance
Ingram Content Group UK Ltd.
Pitfield, Milton Keynes, MK11 3LW, UK
UKHW041902190726
13854UKWH00003B/1036